Life in Ancient Greece

by Noah Leatherland

Minneapolis, Minnesota

Credits
Images are courtesy of Shutterstock.com. With thanks to Getty Images, Thinkstock Photo, and iStockphoto. COVER & RECURRING – Andrei Stepanov, JORDEN MARBLE, Nsit, Macrovector. 4–5 – SCStock, vkilikov. 6–7 – dinosmichail, Mazerath. 8–9 – Lucian Milasan, Zwiebackesser. 10–11 – Jean-Léon Gérôme, Public domain, via Wikimedia Commons, Authentic travel, lemono. 12–13 – Tim UR, aaltair, NotionPic. 14–15 – Steve Swayne, CC BY-SA 2.0 <https://creativecommons.org/licenses/by-sa/2.0>, via Wikimedia Commons, INTREEGUE Photography, Valentyn Volkov. 16–17 – ONYXprj, Uwe Bergwitz, Gilmanshin, baldezh. 18–19 – Cavan-Images, Dima Moroz. 20–21 – garanga, Fabio Alcini. 22–23 – Getty Villa, CC BY-SA 2.0 <https://creativecommons.org/licenses/by-sa/2.0>, via Wikimedia Commons, l i g h t p o e t, National Archaeological Museum of Athens, Public domain, via Wikimedia Commons, johavel. 24–25 – yiannisscheidt, Vadym Sh. 26–27 – Ververidis Vasilis, AngelaLouwe. 28–29 – Zwiebackesser, Nejdet Duzen, inspiring.team, Steinar. 30 – mapman.

Bearport Publishing Company Product Development Team
Publisher: Jen Jenson; Director of Product Development: Spencer Brinker; Managing Editor: Allison Juda; Editor: Cole Nelson; Associate Editor: Naomi Reich; Associate Editor: Tiana Tran; Art Director: Colin O'Dea; Designer: Kim Jones; Designer: Kayla Eggert; Product Development Specialist: Owen Hamlin

Library of Congress Cataloging-in-Publication Data is available at www.loc.gov or upon request from the publisher.

ISBN: 979-8-89232-881-4 (hardcover)
ISBN: 979-8-89232-967-5 (paperback)
ISBN: 979-8-89232-911-8 (ebook)

© 2025 BookLife Publishing
This edition is published by arrangement with BookLife Publishing.

North American adaptations © 2025 Bearport Publishing Company. All rights reserved. No part of this publication may be reproduced in whole or in part, stored in any retrieval system, or transmitted in any form or by any means, electronic, mechanical, photocopying, recording, or otherwise, without written permission from the publisher.

For more information, write to Bearport Publishing, 5357 Penn Avenue South, Minneapolis, MN 55419.

 # CONTENTS

Ancient Greece 4
Gods and Goddesses 6
Cruel Myths 8
Thoughtful Philosophers 10
Health and Sickness 12
The Olympic Games 14
Pretty Greeks 16
Break a Leg 18
Painters and Decorators 20
Playing Games 22
Shocks at Sparta 24
Down in the Underworld 28
Your Place in History 30
Glossary 31
Index 32
Read More 32
Learn More Online 32

ANCIENT GREECE

Life in ancient Greece was full of rich history . . . and baffling behavior! Looking back, some of the stories we hear from ancient Greece may seem strange.

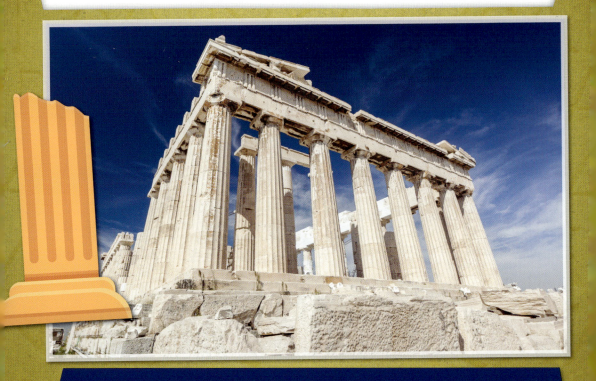

The long history of ancient Greece went from around 1200 BCE to 323 BCE. Ancient Greece was made up of separated areas of land called poleis.

BCE MEANS BEFORE THE COMMON ERA. THIS IS THE TIME BEFORE THE YEAR 0.

Although ancient Greece was split into poleis, the people shared a culture. They spoke the same language, and many believed in the same gods and goddesses. Still, the poleis sometimes went to war with one another.

Athens was an important polis. In 507 BCE, the leaders of Athens set up the world's first democracy. It was a system that let **citizens** vote for their leaders.

GODS AND GODDESSES

Ancient Greeks believed different gods and goddesses were linked to different parts of life. People believed the gods could protect or punish them.

MOUNT OLYMPUS

The most important gods were thought to live at the top of Mount Olympus. The mountain is about 9,570 feet (2,920 m) high. Ancient Greeks claimed the gods could look down on people from up there.

In ancient Greece, the gods were a part of everyday life. People often said prayers or **worshipped** them in other ways. People held festivals to celebrate the gods, too.

A TEMPLE

Temples were also built to worship the gods. The ancient Greeks believed that in these temples priests could receive messages from the gods.

CRUEL MYTHS

Many ancient Greek **myths** were about the gods punishing people. Some of these punishments could even last forever.

PROMETHEUS

In one myth, a man named Prometheus was said to have stolen fire from the gods. Zeus, the king of the gods, punished Prometheus by chaining him to a rock. Every day, an eagle pecked Prometheus open and ate part of his insides!

According to another myth, Sisyphus was a cruel king who tried to trick the gods. So, Zeus punished him. Sisyphus was forced to push a boulder up a mountain. But every time he got near the top, the boulder rolled back down.

SISYPHUS

Another legend said King Tantalus was punished for stealing food while dining with the gods. Every time he reached for food, the wind would blow it away from him!

Thoughtful Philosophers

There were many philosophers in ancient Greece. Philosophers were people who thought about the world and how things worked. Some had strange beliefs about life.

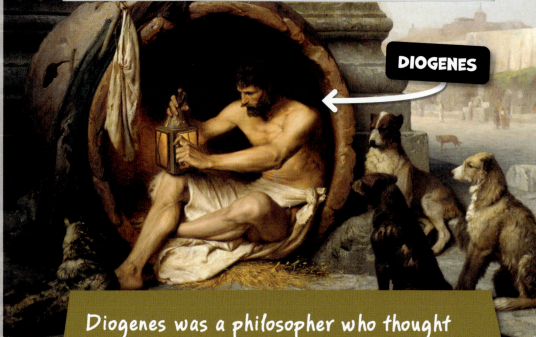

DIOGENES

Diogenes was a philosopher who thought people should live close to nature. He walked around barefoot, lived inside a barrel, and peed and pooped in the street. *Ew!*

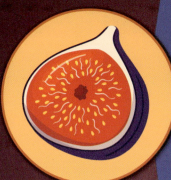

Another thinker, Chrysippus, believed people should always have self-control. However, some stories say that he died laughing at his own joke about a donkey eating a fig.

Hippocrates claimed there were four humors in the body that controlled how a person felt. These **liquids** were blood, **phlegm**, black **bile**, and yellow bile. If someone's humors were not balanced, they would feel sick.

HEALTH AND SICKNESS

Hippocrates's four humors guided how doctors treated people. Doctors believed headaches were caused by people having too much blood. So, Greek doctors cut open their patients to let some of the blood out.

Garlic was thought to **cure** eye problems in ancient Greece. Some doctors told people to put garlic on their eyelids. However, other doctors thought eating garlic would just make people fart.

Ancient Greek doctors used the sense of taste to learn more about someone's humors. They would lick a sick person's vomit to find out what was happening inside their body. Yuck!

DO NOT TRY THIS YOURSELF!

Another way doctors checked their patients' health was by tasting their pee! Doctors thought that if the person was healthy, their pee would taste like fig juice.

THE OLYMPIC GAMES

The Olympic Games were invented by the ancient Greeks. They were held in Olympia. Athletes competed in the games to honor the gods and goddesses of Mount Olympus.

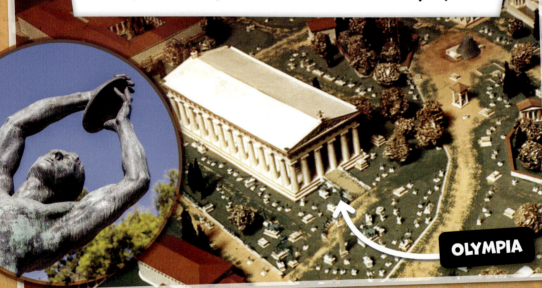

OLYMPIA

Olympic athletes competed in many different events. These included running, jumping, chariot racing, discus throwing, wrestling, and boxing. Most of the athletes competed completely naked!

Ancient Greeks believed that Olympic athlete sweat had special powers. Before they exercised, the athletes were covered in olive oil. Competing would make them sweaty and dirty. After competitions, the dirty, sweaty oil was scraped off athletes and sold as medicine.

THE MIX OF OLIVE OIL, SWEAT, AND DIRT WAS CALLED GLOIOS.

PRETTY GREEKS

Beauty was important in ancient Greece. People made a cream out of crocodile poop to keep their skin wrinkle-free. They thought sitting in bathtubs full of mud and crocodile poop also helped their skin.

A unibrow was a sign of being smart. So, some ancient Greek women gave themselves unibrows using a black powder called soot.

The ancient Greeks found a way to turn their hair blond. First, they washed their hair in a special ointment. Then, they dried their hair in the sun.

Gods and heroes were usually shown in art with big, curly beards. Men in ancient Greece wanted to look just as cool as them. Some even heated metal tongs to use to curl their beards.

BREAK A LEG

Every year, the ancient Greeks held a festival to celebrate the god Dionysus. The festival was held in Athens. Thousands of people gathered in theaters, also called odeums, to watch plays.

Back then, only men were allowed to act in plays. They wore masks and tall shoes on stage. This helped people seated farther back in the audience see them.

There were two types of plays in ancient Greece. Tragedies were serious plays where bad or sad things happened. In *Oedipus the King*, the character Oedipus ends up killing his father and accidentally marrying his mother!

Comedies were funny plays where silly things happened. The actors often wore baffling outfits to make themselves look even sillier.

PAINTERS AND DECORATORS

Ancient Greeks loved to make beautiful things and decorate the places where they lived.

Phidias was a famous sculptor. He made a giant statue of Zeus for the god's temple in Olympia. The statue was 39 ft. (12 m) tall and sat on a throne made of gold and ivory. People traveled from all over to see it.

The ancient Greeks loved to make pots. They painted their pots with scenes from stories about their gods.

For some, pots had a different use. Pots were cheap, so some ancient Greeks used them to wipe their butts! They broke the pots into pieces to scrape their behinds clean. Ouch!

PLAYING GAMES

The ancient Greeks made toys, too. Many toys were made from a type of clay called terracotta.

Ancient Greeks played with toys similar to yo-yos. They painted pictures of gods and goddesses on the sides of their yo-yos. Dolls were another common toy. They often made rattling noises to scare evil spirits away.

Some ancient Greek games are like the ones we have today. Episkyros was a ball game similar to hockey. Players had to get the ball over the other team's line to win.

SCULPTURES IN ANCIENT GREECE OFTEN SHOWED NAKED PEOPLE. SOME BELIEVED IT WAS A SIGN OF STRENGTH.

When children got older, they gave their toys away. Some kids even took their old toys to temples and gave them to the gods.

23

SHOCKS AT SPARTA

Sparta was one of the poleis in ancient Greece. Its warriors were famous for being tough and **brutal**. Spartans did some strange things to make their people strong.

Most Spartans started strength training at a young age. Some myths claim that babies were sometimes left outside to see if they were strong enough to survive.

In ancient Greece, most girls were not allowed to do many of the things that boys did. But in Sparta, the people thought that all children had to be strong.

Girls in Sparta were taught how to wrestle and play sports. They also learned how to sing, dance, and play instruments.

Spartan boys went to a special school called an agoge. There, they trained to become soldiers. However, life in an agoge was tough.

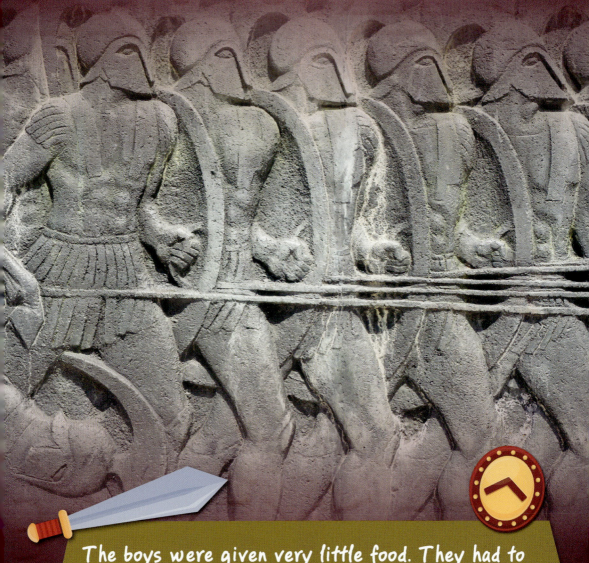

The boys were given very little food. They had to sneak out and steal to have enough to eat. But if the boys got caught, the trainers would punish them.

Boys from Sparta were told tales to **inspire** them.

One story was about a Spartan boy who found a fox after sneaking out. He put the fox under his shirt to hide it from a trainer. The fox scratched him, but the brave boy acted as if it did not hurt.

DOWN IN THE UNDERWORLD

Ancient Greeks believed in an **afterlife**. To get there, the dead had to cross the River Styx. They had to pay a ferryman named Charon.

CHARON

The ancient Greeks buried their dead with a coin. This was so the dead could pay Charon. Those who could not pay were believed to wander hopelessly for 100 years.

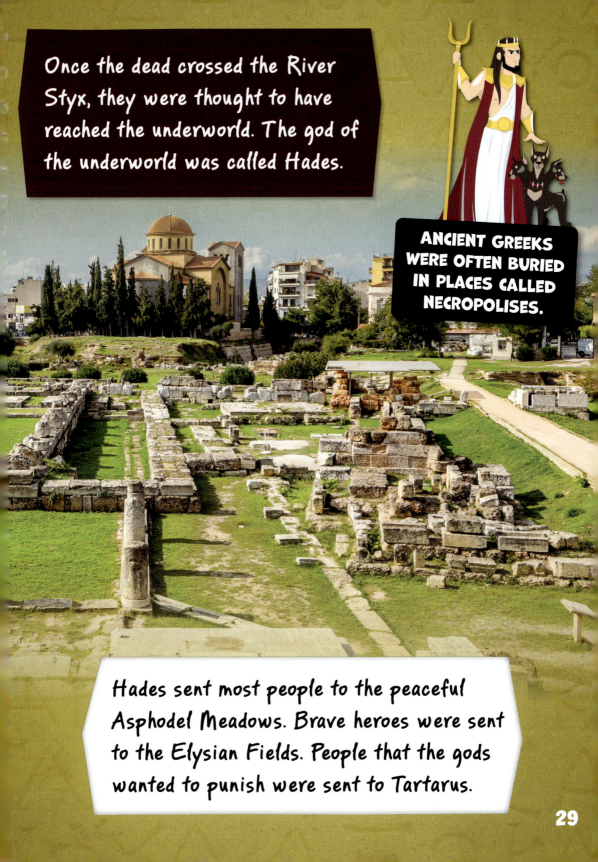

Once the dead crossed the River Styx, they were thought to have reached the underworld. The god of the underworld was called Hades.

ANCIENT GREEKS WERE OFTEN BURIED IN PLACES CALLED NECROPOLISES.

Hades sent most people to the peaceful Asphodel Meadows. Brave heroes were sent to the Elysian Fields. People that the gods wanted to punish were sent to Tartarus.

YOUR PLACE IN HISTORY

Do you think you could live in ancient Greece? From training as a Spartan to wiping your butt with broken pots, the people who lived in the past sure had it rough.

If you think being in ancient Greece was tough, then try reading about another time period. However, be warned! Wherever you go, you may find yourself thinking . . .

what baffling behavior!

GLOSSARY

afterlife the life of a person after their death

bile a yellowish or dark-green fluid in the liver that helps break down food

brutal extremely tough or difficult

citizens people who live in a particular country, city, or town

cure to get rid of an illness completely

inspire to influence or encourage someone to do something

liquids materials that flow, such as water

myths traditional stories that may or may not be true

phlegm a thick substance that can be found in the lungs and is often coughed up during a cold

worshipped honored and respected as a god

INDEX

Athens 5, 18	**plays** 18–19
athletes 14–15	**pots** 21, 30
doctors 12–13	**Spartans** 24–27, 30
figs 11, 13	**temples** 7, 20, 23
hair 17	**vomit** 13
Mount Olympus 6, 14	**Zeus** 8–9, 20
pee 10, 13	

READ MORE

Mather, Charis. *The Peculiar Past in Ancient Greece (Strange History).* Minneapolis: Bearport Publishing Company, 2024.

Troupe, Thomas Kingsley. *Brutal Spartans (Ancient Warriors).* New York: Crabtree Publishing, 2024.

LEARN MORE ONLINE

1. Go to **FactSurfer.com** or scan the QR code below.

2. Enter "**Life in Ancient Greece**" into the search box.

3. Click on the cover of this book to see a list of websites.